MW01463129

# GARRETT GREEN

## A Revolutionary Mind: How My Family, Friends, & PTSD Would Shape Me

## Vol. I

J. Garrett Green

www.JGarrettGreen.com

**An Autobiography by J. Garrett Green**

This book was authored March 17, 2020.

***www.JGarrettGreen.com***

## Foreword

I must begin first by thanking the God of Abraham because I understand God to mean Love. In knowing this, I love all human beings because love resides in each other. The *ability* for one to love is the ability to fulfill the purpose of one's life. Without love, we can be consumed by social conditions that cause us to react in different situations, rather than assessing the circumstances to make conscious decisions.

We must be the creators of our own labels and the writers of our own fate. How can we prepare to live in paradise later, if we are going through hell now? Our current state of mind is a choice. You and I have the power to choose, in the current moment, to be happy or angry. Choosing to be angry at the actions of someone else means *you* chose anger. Choosing happiness gives you *power* to be in control of your emotional self. In which emotions control thoughts, and thoughts control words and actions.

The question is, are the actions of a negative nature or good?

# Table of Contents

# Chapter One

## Before the Beginning

I was born on October 10, 1986 in a local hospital in Pensacola, Florida, at 6:28 a.m. My mother (DeMina "DeeDee" Green) and father (Raymond Strother) were never married. My older sister is Tiffany, along with 3 additional sisters through my father, not raised in my household.

My mother, Tiffany, and I lived with my maternal grandparents. This was largely due to medical reasons, and the ability to have a safe and stable home for Tiffany and myself. My grandfather, C.M. Green, was born on August 4, 1929. We call him "DaddyGreen" because my mom and her sisters called their grandfather that name. My DaddyGreen moved from Hopkins, South Carolina to Pensacola because he joined the military, in the late 1940's. Hopkins is a rural community outside of Columbia, South Carolina. DaddyGreen met Gloria Denton, while he was in Pensacola.

DaddyGreen would marry Gloria on October 28, 1950. Gloria, of course, is my maternal grandmother, whom we called "Granny." She was born in the Tan Yard Community (a predominantly Black population) in Pensacola, Florida. Granny was born at her home, on August 10, 1932. However, her birth record reflects her date of birth being August 19, 1932 because it would be 9 days after Granny's birth, before she was taken to the hospital. Granny's mother (Blanche) was a Black store owner, having moved to Pensacola upon turning the age of 18. Blanche moved to Pensacola from Bay Minette, Alabama.

DaddyGreen and Granny had three daughters as a result of their marriage. Vanessa is the oldest, born in 1956. My mom was born second, in 1959. My aunt, Clareta "Baba," was the last child born in 1962. I have incorporated all of these individuals' best qualities, to make them a part of who I am.

In regards to the grandchildren, Baba married and created the first grandchild, Angela Monique, who was born in May of 1982. I have always considered Monique to be like a sister. Monique and I have always shared a creative way of thinking. This causes us to see many things that average people do not observe. Also, this is why we have such a unique sense of humor. Ultimately, we lock eyes after our unique observations, trying to hold our laughter in, which often leads to failure.

Monique has understood my personality since childhood. Her leaving to join the military caused me confusion, not because of her decision to leave, but we communicated less often. I could not understand why. Yet, when we did talk or see each other, there was never love lost. We are each on our own journey. And honestly, I had a responsibility to reciprocate that communication too.

Tiffany was born in November of 1982. Like all big sisters, she loved to torment me. But it was childhood torment, we grew out of our childish ways. Tiffany has been the overprotective sister of a brother who can adequately fight his own battles. It is funny to sit back and watch at times.

Tiffany's actions were out of love, although unnecessary at times. I believe she takes my calm demeanor for weakness, although not intentionally. I have always admired her love of life, with disregard of the opinion of others, although this trait can also lead to trouble. Tiffany has always been good at steering clear of major troubles though.

Then, I come along in October of 1986. The only man-child of the maternal children and grandchildren; along with being the only (known) man-child of my father. I am blessed to have been granted the circumstances I was granted, given the history of my family, in particularly; and the history of Black people, in general, in this country.

The struggle and plight of the African diaspora within the United States has been and continues to be built on systems of injustice. The disregard to justice is a disregard to "certain unalienable rights granted by our Creator, that every human being be granted life, freedom, and the ability to pursue happiness."

The historical and racial injustices associated with my immediate familial line and Black people, throughout time, gives my life purpose. Injustices my people have lived through fuel me to seek justice, by any legal means necessary; now and for the future.

## Chapter Two

## Younger Years

Many of my childhood memories were with DaddyGreen. I recall my first time going fishing at the age of 3, I threw my fishing pole in the water at the feel of a nibble on the other end of the line. After I threw the pole, I knew DaddyGreen would be furious because he had just given me that red fishing pole. However, that day, he showed me something that he showed me and others often... patience.

DaddyGreen packed everything up, assuring me everything was okay. We drove home, about ten minutes, which seemed forever. Once home, he goes to the shed, gets another pole, and rigs it with heavy weights and a huge hook. After rigging the pole, we drive back to the fishing spot, he casts the line, and drags the rig across the area I threw the pole. Amazingly he recovered my red fishing pole. At 3 years old, that was the coolest thing ever.

Even now, it still is amazing because I realize how patience would help me throughout life. DaddyGreen showed me, through patience, that there was a solution to a problem, if one takes the time to think. Many of my life's lessons would come, like most people, through experience. However, life would not always be so kind and forgiving.

I started pre-school at Jehovah Lutheran, around the same age. However, I was always raised in the

Catholic Church, having generational family history at St. Joseph's Catholic Church. St. Joseph's was the first Black Catholic Church in the State of Florida, opened after the Reconstruction Era, during the Jim Crow South, in the early 1890s.

Religion would influence many decisions in my life, until the point I had to lose it to find God, and myself. At the age of 4, I began kindergarten at Pensacola Christian School because I would be turning 5 the upcoming October. Looking back, I did not like Pensacola Christian School at all. Even during the kindergarten and the first grade years I was there, they (1.) showed us pictures of a white Jesus, (2.) I got a "D" on a quiz in the 1st grade, and (3.) no one could walk swinging their arms. I was sent to the back of the lunch line for walking in a natural motion.

Even more, Pensacola Christian School is where I would first recall questioning myself. It was not a question of "who" was I? Rather, it was a question of "what" was I?" More-so, "what was I 'mixed' with?" This questioning of my Blackness would be a source of conflict within myself because I always had something to prove.

Yet, in the 1st grade, my best friend Marcus would help me conclude, on the bus, I must be like Michael Jackson because he and I were both black, but our skin was light. Marcus and I kindly went on about our day.

Upon finishing 1st grade, my mom sent Tiffany and me to St. Michael's Catholic School. Tiffany would be starting 6th grade, and I would be starting the 2nd grade. St. Michael's had the highest Black population of all of the Catholic Schools in the area, grades K-8. However, we were still a large minority.

I was always into religion class. This was based on my looking on a map, seeing the geographic region of Jesus and the "Chosen People." This was Africa. Jesus and the people in this region are Black. This was my frame of mind. I enjoyed this state of mind because I was Black, and it is something indeed to be proud. Religion class and going to church excited me because I was learning about Black history.

I knew the stories of the Bible very well, at a young age. My $8^{th}$ grade art teacher thought I was painting something demonic when I painted a scene of St. Peter being crucified for continuing to spread the Word of the Gospel, after Jesus' death. She did not know he requested to be crucified upside down because he did not feel worthy enough to be crucified in the same manner as Jesus. Of course, she became enlightened in a conference with my religion teacher, who confirmed this as being a biblical story.

Most of my conflicts with teachers came from questions I asked. My mom allowed me to have the choice of going to Booker T. Washington High School or Pensacola Catholic High School. I chose Booker T. Washington High School.

I was tired of going to catholic school, and wanted to be around more Black people. Also, my grandmother went to Booker T. Washington, although she never finished her last year because someone stole her only sweater, during the winter. Granny always told me to "never let someone stop you from getting your education. If you think you can do it, you can. You got it." With an encouraging smile and thumbs up.

So, I was going to be a wildcat! Since I was anticipating playing football, I enrolled in summer school, before my freshman year. I took gym, to be able to lift weights and have something to do, so that I was not at home. Also, there were going to be more girls than there ever were at St. Michael's.

While at summer school, we got to lift weights and play different sports. I do not recall who gave me the name, during one pick-up game of basketball, but the name "Elian" stuck for some time. I rolled with it early on because it was a way for me to be remembered by people. People remembered because this was during a time when Elian Gonzalez was on the news, being televised with a gun in his face by the U.S. Government being sent back to Cuba. Now, I attribute our resemblance to our ethnicities responsible for our cultures being in the Americas, along with the African roots of our ethnic diaspora. In essence, Black People come in all shades.

Booker T. Washington High School had the capacity to challenge my intellect, had I let it be known the majority of my classes were too easy. However, I would do the amount of work required to pass to my satisfaction. In the 10th grade, I remember walking into school, being dropped off by Granny, and being immediately instructed to the gym for something call the "FCAT."

I had no idea what the FCAT entailed, until I sat down and read the cover of the scan-tron, the "Florida Comprehensive Assessment Test." Although I did not know what the test was for, or anything about the test, I was glad to be out of class. Afterwards, I would not think much about the FCAT. Sometime later, I got the results saying I passed the FCAT and I did not have to retake it to graduate high school.

10th Grade was the only time I ever got into "real" trouble at school. Another kid on the football team, an 11th grader, would always pick on me, even though I bothered no one. I would always defend myself well and had many friends who would not allow anyone else to bother me, seeing as how I weighed about 100 pounds.

On a normal day of class, going to weightlifting, which was required for football players, the boy jumped on my back and hit me in the head. I slung him over my shoulder to get him off of me. During weightlifting class, I noticed his cousin was not there. His cousin would often intervene when I defended myself from the boy's offensive acts. During weightlifting class, I gathered several of my friends and associates to "get" the boy back for hitting me in my head.

Once in the locker-room, our horseplay resulted in us carrying the boy around. He ultimately, ended feet-up in the disgusting, football locker-room trashcan. As a result of this, the star running-back and I were suspended. Additionally, we had to take anger management classes. This was the only time I was ever involved in any mischief that resulted in academic discipline.

That summer, going to the 11th grade, my mom got a call about my FCAT scores. My mom came outside, where I was, saying "someone from the school district called. You scored in the 98th percentile, and they want to know if you wanted to change your classes." I simply responded "no." There was no further conversation on the matter.

Honestly, I was satisfied getting by. Also, I thought being in the 98th percentile was a bad thing. I always wanted to be number one.

During my junior and senior years, people still called me "Elian." However, by this time, I referred to myself in the third person. It was partly due to an air about myself, and largely due to rebranding myself from being "Elian" to being me.

This would not be the last time I would have to redefine who I am because of labels given to me. But, at this time, I did not understand how to define myself through having knowledge of self. My need, to redefine myself, often comes from outgrowing old patterns of thinking.

My best friend throughout high school (and to this day) was Antonio. He has always been like a brother to me, and we got into a great deal of tomfoolery. Antonio and I went to St. Joseph's together, and were in the same church youth group.

In May of 2004, I graduated from Booker T. Washington High

School. That August, I left for Mobile, Alabama to attend the University of South Alabama at age 17. My college experience, coupled with the foundation of God and family would take me on a trying journey. A journey, which my younger years would have prepared me for to be tried spiritually, emotionally, mentally, and physically. Yet, I would not learn this until well after the fact.

# Chapter Three

## College Days: A Different World

My college experience is one that would have a great influence on my life, during a pivotal developmental stage. I was like any young man on a college campus. I started with a college major in engineering. My first semester was full of prerequisites. I had a 3.25 GPA after that first semester. My godfather always represented Kappa Alpha Psi Fraternity, Inc., well. With a 3.25 GPA, and 15 credits, I was able to pledge this fraternity during my second semester of college. However, I attribute my ignorance as to why I succumbed to the peer pressure of my pledge process to being 18 years old at the time.

Members of the organization would test your willingness to pledge by having one do menial tasks, until it was decided you were worthy enough to pledge on-line. My pledge process lasted a total of sixty (60) consecutive days, without any leisure time. Hours to meet began at 9:00 p.m., lasting until at least 2:00 a.m., if not longer. Returning to my dorm room as the sun rises was not a rare occurrence. The length of time depended on my line's perfection of harmonious recitation of "knowledge." Knowledge was always good. A nightly session could easily consist of twenty (20) big brothers, on average. To begin the session, we had to greet our big brothers. Part of greeting the big brothers was "taking wood." Taking wood occurred often. My chapter started with a wooden cane and ended with a wooden cane; as opposed to others stories of organizations using paddles or boat oars.

While on-line I was 5'11" and weighed 135 pounds. Yet, I was the "rock" of my line. Being the rock is a title held proudly by many, yet only one person on each line could be a rock. It meant a person got hit with the wood the best, without breaking cut or wincing.

Our routine in shop consisted of taking wood from any of the numerous brothers present, who wanted to be shown "love," or wanted to show love to their little "brothers." To many of us, the pledge process is a rite of passage, a journey to help one grow and bond between individuals. I would grow to learn of its more harmful effects.

Another way to get wood was a catch 22. Spitting knowledge to perfection would cause you to get in the cut for being too perfect. Messing up meant taking 3 licks. Simply put, one could not escape going into the cut.

Messing up would occur often because of the physical and mental pressures inflicted. Yet we were to excel beyond this endeavor because "pain is temporary, pride is forever."

There are many other instances of the physical and mental torment, but the "wood" was most memorable. Also, this is evident by the large scar on my right butt cheek.

Ironically, the physical pain did not bother me much. The mental games affected me most. Our seventh week into the process was my absolute breaking point while on-line. As the rock, my right buttock had begun to separate, which was caused by the indentation caused from the impact of the wooden cane.

When a pledge was hit with a cane, it was often with the cane gripped like a baseball bat. The cane was often swung with the same force one would use to swing a baseball bat. A cane breaking was not a rare occurrence either.

One of our "easier" nights consisted of only six or seven big brothers. Two of the big brothers had never "seen" us on-line, asking "who is the rock?" My dean of pledges pointed with his cane. The two brothers were in utter shock and awe when they saw the scrawny guy, who did not look "Black," and finding out he was the rock of his line. It was me.

Due to their disbelief, it was resolved they would have a contest. The contest consisted of attempting to "break" me out of the "cut." Another big brother placed a beer-bottle cap onto the top of my head. There were two (2) criterion, and we could go home: (1.) do not break cut; and (2.) do not let the bottle cap fall off of my head. If one of the criteria were unmet, we would be in shop until a time to be determined.

For 15-20 minutes, three brothers, including the two (2)

disbelieving brothers, rotated hitting me with a cane, 3 licks at a time. After this period of time, my dean of pledges called for "brothers off line." I believe he had sympathy and empathy for what I had just endured.

"Brothers off line," was an understood safety phrase. The only other words my dean of pledges said were, "Enough. Get back in." This earned our ability to leave shop early that night. An early departure was a rare occurrence. In order to leave shop, each of my line brothers, and myself, had to take three (3) licks from each brother to leave. That night, a few brothers showed mercy, in the lack of force when it came to be my turn. Another rare occurrence.

However, a few “lucky” nights happened for us while on-line. During a particular part of the process, we were being inducted into a club. Later, things were going to be extremely amped up. We had to wear dress slacks. Of the many canes present, all were broken on my line and I, in the first 15-minutes of the night’s session. Our chapter used paddles as decoration. A paddle on the wall would be used next, but it dissatisfied brothers swinging the paddle. We went home slightly earlier that night. Going home early was a sign of luck.

My line name is T.K.O. It does have an actual meaning but the reason behind the name is due to the several occasions I blacked out. We would be standing in our formation for so long, my legs would lock. I would get tunnel vision, as the room would go black.

There are many different stories, but the point is the mental effects of the various beatings, and mental infliction of harm that occurred within and upon me (among many others). The total number of days of my pledge process was sixty (60). It was pure torment. April through June of 2005 was the amount of time it took before the scab fell off my buttock, and it took June until August to "heal." A Scar, where my skin reconnected and the look of a chunk of flesh missing are my physical reminders of my process, which would remain with me until this day. I would not realize the extent of the psychological effects until later.

After I crossed on April 2, 2005 at 12:32am, my college experience intensified. The connections I would make would give me access to vast arrays of college scenes. This was due to the number of road trips. We would go to parties, meet girls, drink alcohol, and smoke weed. Going to class was the easiest thing I could do, but I stopped going to class.

I realized I was messing up, and my mom checking me soon after, assisted me changing my frame of mind. The fall semester of 2006, I set on a path to prove not only to my mom and others, but to myself, that I could be successful in my academic pursuits. I would not see what would soon come….

## Chapter Four

## <u>College Days: A Heavy Burden</u>

August 2006 could not come fast enough. I set my mind to reading biblical scriptures, doing homework, and still trying to create more friendships with college ladies. However, the flesh is still weak, and I often found myself under the advances of those friends. In that day, in that frame of mind, I was conflicted but I did not mind.

I thought every person has at least one vice, and my promiscuity was my vice. I began putting more effort into not letting this vice, or any vice, control me. With this effort, it seemed more ladies would approach me.

I do remember, this was the year Alexandria would get to the university. She was always a good friend throughout the years. Having always maintained a level of respect, never having crossed into a more intimate relationship.

During my promiscuity, I was known to be an "asshole" because of my blunt persona, which was and is very direct and matter-of-fact. I found this sense of honesty to be what I needed to continue on my life's journey, while learning my place in this world. I did not want to be that religious scripture hollering person, denouncing every action of a person. In my frame of thinking, Jesus spoke *with* regular people, not really preaching, rather relating. Jesus had a Light people naturally inquired about.

I knew my light was shining but did not understand how to use it.

I felt a sense of *grandiose* with the knowledge of the Word I had. Not realizing that on this October 3rd, of 2006, I had not been to sleep in a few days. My body simply was not sleepy nor was I tired. One night, something told me to call home. I did, which Tiffany answered. I asked if she loved God, and she replied "yes." I said "I love you too." I had no sense of time, as I simply hung up after 1:00 am, saying "bye." My family and doctors would believe I was grandiose, from this statement. However, what I meant by my reply, was that since she loved God, I was able to love her. The 19 year old me, was not as eloquent as now.

On October 6, 2006, as dawn approached, I dressed and left my dorm room in the Gamma Residence Hall Area on the university's campus. When I departed, I left behind my wallet. I got into my SUV, and drove to the house of my fraternity/line brother's mother. I went there because I would frequent there often, as I would pick him up from his mother's home as we would embark on various shenanigans.

My line brother's mother was walking out of her home as I was pulling into the driveway. I got out asking where her son was located? Her reply "Jonathan, you know Brandon is at work, he did not tell you?" She stood with a puzzled look of confusion upon her face. I should have known this already.

I got into my SUV, leaving with no particular destination. I then saw a fire truck, with lights and sirens on, at a red light. The location of the red light was near the interstate, which there was a sign that read "Pensacola;" thus, I decided to drive home.

I got onto I-10 East, going over 100 miles per hour. After driving for about thirty minutes, I passed a red Honda, disabled outside a town named Loxley, Alabama (Exit 44). I felt someone may be in distress, so I stopped. There was no one inside or outside of the Honda. At this point I began driving in the emergency lane, against the flow of traffic.

Shortly after, a member of the Loxley police department pulled in front of my SUV, with lights on, all while on I-10. The officers was exiting his vehicle, so I exited my SUV. As we approached each 0ther, he asked in a very stereotypical, southern accent "what are you doing?"

I responded, "Do you know who *I Am*?" He replied "who are you?" in a frantic voice, as a physical tussle ensued. During this time period, this particular officer did not have a taser, to my belief, I could have easily been shot. In my mind, this situation led back to the question I asked my sister that early morning…"do you love God?" My reply of "I love you too," was because I considered myself a child of God. So when I asked the officer if he knew who I was, I rhetorically was referring to myself as a child of God.

The basis of the aggression, I attribute to Stockholm Syndrome. Having assimilated with an oppressor who has no right to have authority over me. Also, I considered him and the other white-male corrections and police officers to be "blue-eyed devils," although I would lose this philosophy.

During the scuffle, another officer approached, although I did not see him approaching us. The three (3) of us struggled until I was caught with a foot swipe. My chin was split on the pavement, as they handcuffed me. My button-up shirt came off during the struggle, hanging on to me by my right arm. The officers placed me in the back of the patrol car, without a thorough search.

While the officers stood, talking, and attempting to figure out what in the hell just happened, I took a lighter out of my pocket. Once the lighter was in hand, I took the left sleeve of my shirt, not attached to my person, and set the sleeve on fire. My supposed intent was to try to take the police car, if I was able to escape the back of the patrol car.

I was able to set my shirt ablaze because I stepped over my handcuffs, reached in my pocket, and set the left-shirt sleeve on fire. At this time, at place the small blaze on the far right side of the police car, and I sat on the extreme left. I began yelling "fire!" repeatedly like a "mad man."

By this time there were 5 or 6 police officers present, which they all appeared frantic. They got me out of the patrol car, but I did not anticipate I would not escape their grasp once out of the police car. One of the officers got a fire extinguisher out of his trunk, and stops the small fire.

At this point, the officers are asking me questions, and I am replying repeatedly, "babble on." I said this phrase as a play on words for "Babylon." The officers asked where I was heading. I responded "East," although I would not know why for some years later.

Once the situation is controlled, the officers take me to the Loxley Police Department to await transport to the Baldwin County Jail.

## Chapter Five

## College Days: The Day in Jail

The altercation on I-10 happened around the nine (9) o'clock hour, in the morning. While in the Baldwin County Jail, a Detention Officer bumped me as he walked by me. I told him, "Excuse you." He replied, very condescendingly, "What did you say?" This prompted my saying, "you heard me you blue-eyed devil, I will spit on your ass!" His foolish reply was "I dare you."

Fulfilling his dare got me placed into the restraint chair with the quickness. The chair was made of metal and plastic, while the straps were of the same nature and material as seatbelts in cars. After several hours in the restraint chair, I managed to get the spit bag and helmet off my head, while restrained.

The guards moved the chair between two doors, to stop my ability to spit on the white, blue-eyed, male guards.  After several more hours, and still no sleep for days, and sitting in the restraint chair, I was able to work the straps enough to be able to slide one of my arms out of the restraints.

Once, there was slack in the strap, the rest of the straps essentially fall off.  As I was taking the last strap off my left leg, the guards ran in; snatching me up and placing me into another restraint chair with shackles. A guard performed a sleeper move on me numerous times for the other guards to work, during my resistance.

My wrist and ankles became swollen from the amount of time I was shackled. In that time period, I urinated on myself because I was not allowed to be free. Also, I still had not eaten since about October 3rd, which was also the last day I had any amount of sleep.

A little after 6:00 a.m., I was able to make a phone call and have my mugshot taken. Tiffany answered the house phone, saying our mom and Baba had just located me, and were trying to bail me out. It turns out, my dean of pledges, who took Physics: Astronomy with me, came to my dorm so we could go to class together, per usual. But it was unusual that my dorm was unlocked, and even more so, that my wallet was present. Also, my keys were missing, and I was no where to be found.  Somewhere along the way to Pensacola, I threw my phone out the window, of my SUV, as I saw my dean of pledges calling.

He was seeing if I was ready for class.  He noticed my behavior had been strange.  His attempts to get my family's phone number were not successful.  The residence hall sent my family into a panic when my family was called with an inquiry if I was in Pensacola.  My family responded I should be at the University.  My dean of pledges actions caused my family to act, when the residence hall called my family.  Their actions and due diligence allowed them to eventually find me in the Baldwin County Jail, to be able to post the bail.

## Chapter Six

## The Bail Out

My general attitude towards white people, and people in general, has changed immensely since the time of my police interaction of 2006. However, as I was walking out of the Baldwin County Jail, I yelled "go back to hell you blue-eyed devils." My mother and aunt's expressions were priceless, and full of fear, as they ushered me into their car. I signed my bond paperwork, then they rushed me to a hospital in Pensacola.

At this time, I was labeled/diagnosed as suffering a manic bi-polar episode. I would spend the next eleven days hospitalized. Family were daily visitors, and fraternity brothers visited too. As I grew older, I look at how much of a blessing it was those police officers in Loxley, Alabama did not kill me. In the same breath, I used to torment myself. I would constantly ask God, “why he would place such a heavy mental challenge and burden on me, at such a young age?” I ask this, as I endure this burden every day.

I do look at this incident as a blessing, a bail out of my old ways, to have a fresh vision. This is because nothing is placed onto a person, more than the amount which one can bear. It was an honor for me that I told God to use me to fulfill the purpose *He* has for my life. I made this proclamation, at a church service, in June of 2006. My *Creator* tested my faith to see if I would be *True* to my word to *Him*.

This outlook and view would remain to this day.

## Chapter Seven

## Return to the South...Alabama

After a medical leave of absence, from the University of South Alabama, I would return the fall semester of 2007. There were a lot of rumors I heard about myself. One was that I took ecstasy pills. Another was that I thought I was Jesus, and the police found me naked, in a ditch, while holding a bible. All of these stories were untrue, but the whispers were loud.

I started to transfer to the University of Central Florida, but I felt I had something to prove by returning to the University of South Alabama. I had to finish from USA, to prove the story-tellers wrong. I would not be defeated.

I would meet some of my closest friends through the fraternity, which caused me so much pain and grief. Garry, Calvin, Tim, Tristan, Shamil, and I had an even more unique bond. They pledged the fraternity in 2007. Calvin, Garry, Tristan, and I earned our undergraduate degrees in 2009, while Shamil and Tim graduated in 2010.

## Chapter Eight

## Wake-Up, Work, Play, Sleep, Repeat

Life after undergraduate graduation was typical of the college graduate of my generation. Complete your degree, with an expectation of making no less than $60,000 because "I am worth it." The issue would be, everyone with a bachelor's degree is worth it too.

I began working for a non-profit program, responsible for clients adjudicated to juvenile probation. I made a little more than $10.00/hour, being one of the two residential case managers. The primary offenses revolved around substance abuse and behavioral issues. I loved this job, the pay just was not sufficient; however, this is the life of social services. I believed the best thing for me was leaving this jobs after 5 months, to work for the Florida Department of Juvenile Justice, as a detention officer. The life of a detention officer was not for me because of the wrongs occurring during my 2 months there. My final report was one of whistle-blowing because I could not tolerate the injustices I witnessed, in the name of maintain the *color of the badge*.

In January of 2011, I was able to regain employment with my previous, non-profit employer, as an outpatient case manager; in Mobile, Alabama. This job was great, and taught me a lesson in job satisfaction over compensation, because one gains valuable experience. Additionally, I had the ability to make a positive impact on my adolescent clients, and work in the field. However, the problem, would be a lack of resources. Once again, welcome to the world of social services.

While working at this non-profit, I finished my coursework for my Master of Science in Criminal Justice, from the Troy University. I worked for the non-profit for a total of 2 years, before leaving to work for the Florida Department of Children and Families (DCF), in April of 2012. I would have my master's degree conferred in May of 2012.

I would often go back to Mobile, Alabama to visit friends. On one particular visit, Alexandria and I decided we should see about our friendship going further. Over time, we would remain friends, until our paths would cross again, some years later….

## Chapter Nine

## <u>Going To Law School</u>

Granny always asked me, since a young age, "What do you want to be when you grow up?" I would most often reply, "A lawyer." I always enjoyed arguing factual points. Many times, I would be correct because I would not engage in an argument unless I already knew the factual answer, not my opinion.

As I grew older, I became more silent to listen more. Yet, the desire to learn the law remained. I would apply to several law schools, but ultimately decided upon attending the Southern University Law Center in Baton Rouge, Louisiana.

Upon going to SULC, I felt mentally mature enough, and mentally prepared for the task at hand. I was glad to be going to a Historically Black College & University, which the motto of the law center is "*Seriousness of Purpose*." At the age of 26, in June of 2013, I would leave Pensacola for law school. At this age, I knew my purpose. By the age of 28, I understood this purpose. Shamil, a good friend from undergraduate, would embark on this law school journey with me.

In July of 2014, I visited my biological father, Raymond, and his family in Orlando, Florida. Tiffany came as well. In a picture of Tiffany and myself, along with two of our half-blood sisters, Staci and Ryan, I was able to truly see myself. I was *humongous*. This occurred in the instance, upon which I saw the picture, after it was taken.

At first sight of that picture, I was disappointed in myself. I told myself I could not love myself, and the way I looked was a testament to my self-love, or lack thereof. The moment I returned to Baton Rouge, and got the opportunity on that Monday, I went to my law school classes, and then to the gym. I made this my daily routine: (1.) Class; (2.) Gym; (3.) Call my grandparents; (4.) Study; (5.) Eat (6.) Sleep; and (7.) Start the routine over.

From the time frame of July 2014 through November 2014, I went from weighing 211 pounds to weighing 175 pounds. That

September, I suffered a concussion playing basketball with some classmates. While going after a loose ball, I caught an elbow to the left-side of my head, in my temple area. My vision went bright white, while a bell constantly rung. This concussion would lead to post-concussion syndrome, and my wearing glasses.

## Chapter Ten

## An Intellectual Challenge

Awkwardly enough, law school was exactly what I needed in life. It provided the mental stimulation I sought, finally. I attribute my mediocre performance, in school, throughout life with becoming bored with various subject matter.

The first year of law school was challenging. My writing skills saved me, and my legal writing scores let me know I should be at the Southern University Law Center, or any law school for that matter. My 2L year, I understood the law, and the law school system. My intellectual abilities were now able to be challenged. Going into my 3L year, I chose three of the hardest professors, and was doing well. However, in November of 2015, I would have another manic episode; causing me to take another medical leave of absence.

I had no intention to harm myself or anyone else. I dressed in a black suit, with my starter locks under a black turban. I had a briefcase filled with "literature," or in other words, law school textbooks.

I went to class as normal, and attempted to sit in the class of another professor, to get an idea of my last semester classes. I asked the administration office, who advised me it was okay for me to sit-in. A white student told the professor I was not supposed to be in the class. The white professor called me to the front, making an inquiry into my person and purpose. He stated I could not sit in his class at an HBCU. The legal reasoning the institution of SULC was opened was for this same essence.

I went to the administration office, where the vice-chancellor of financial affairs was left in charge, due to others teaching or being in meetings. He then directed me to interrupt the Chancellor's class to address the matter. I did.

The chancellor supported the professor after expressing, to me, I should be able to sit in a class. This angered and confused me. "How could you support this? I take my purpose seriously," I declared. I was ready to drop out of law school, and this effectively killed my yearning to learn.

I took off my shirt, coat and tie, and sat on the law center stoop, in a white tank-top, with my briefcase of literature. Word got back to me that some white boys were talking about getting their guns for me because I made them nervous when I told them my briefcase contained "literature," while I staged a protest on the law school stoop. Some of my comrades checked on me, and I told them "trust me."

I did not want to die, but I would that day. The entire concept was based on the principle of the matter. My comrades Ryan, Fatima, and Jamar were legal comrades dedicated to liberation. They recorded scenes of that day on their phones. My family drove to Baton Rouge, picking me up, and I returned to Pensacola on a medical leave of absence.

## Chapter Eleven

## The Story Between the Lines

During this time period, I began a healthier lifestyle because I exercised daily and was a lacto-ovo vegetarian. This meant I did not eat meat, but I did eat products made of dairy and/or eggs. Also, I stopped smoking black and mild cigars. I began thinking extremely clear, and was still well-acquainted with my Holy Scriptures. I stopped drinking alcohol, although I never enjoyed drinking.

Granny had been recently diagnosed with a rare cancer that was in her sinus cavity and growing into her optic nerve. When she was diagnosed, I reminded the family that the only difference between yesterday and today is that we know what is causing Granny's pain. They could not understand why I was smiling at my granny. Based on my own pain and hurt, I knew a sad face of another would be the last thing I would want to see in my own sadness.

I attempted traveling home at least every other weekend during the last year and a half of law school, 4 hours away, for a one-way trip. I believe the law school hazing mixed with my grandmother's illness, and the post-concussion syndrome contributed to my second episode of complex post-traumatic stress disorder, which manifest as bi-polar mania. This episode would occur in November of 2015. Additionally, an ex-girlfriend, during this same time, misinformed me she was pregnant 2 months after our breakup.

It is very likely, these various pressures of the various situations produced the results of this episode. Blessedly, the Chancellor of the law school was very attentive to his students. Also, Shamil was able to help be there for me. We were roommates for the first year and a half of law school, and our friendship always lasted. My time period spent being hospitalized was about seven (7) days during this complex PTSD occurrence. Each of these episodes has revealed an inner truth about myself and others.

After this particular episode of 2015, I considered dropping out of law school, during my final semester.

I continued through the motions. That passion and love, I once had from the challenge and rigor of an intellectual challenge, subsided. The thrill was gone.

The law school hazing process successfully dulled the fire inside of me. Essentially, I was being told I cannot use knowledge in a way other than to assimilate. This does hold true for many. I face the social and economic hardships, as that of many other people. Yet, I viewed the practice of law as continuing to perpetuate an unjust system. Any justice obtained in an unjust system still yields injustice.

My theory is to fix the criminal justice system, to rid ourselves of the need of having to defend. There is not a need for a defense, if there was never an offense of the law. In knowing this purpose, creating a system anew, I began to seek justice in a new way….I developed (with assistance of other law school comrades) "The Legal Theory and Methodology for Liberation."

## Chapter Twelve

## <u>Balance: The Battle Between Good and Bad</u>

March of 2016, Alexandria and I were engaged, after rekindling a spark in our friendship. She would be the one who encouraged me to stay in law school, and finish my last semester. However, I was 2 classes short of earning my degree, after the second manic episode. This caused my graduation to be delayed to the summer, which my degree was conferred on July 22, 2016. Luckily, the courses I needed to graduate were being offered over the summer. A week after finishing my last law school exam, I sat for the Florida Bar exam.

A constant contention of mine was that I did not want to practice law, yet I took the Florida Bar exam because people told me I should. I kept listening to this against my better judgment. I moved back to Pensacola with a pregnant fiancé, after taking the bar exam.

About a week later, on August 7, 2016, Granny passed away after her battle with that rare type of cancer. It makes me laugh now, thinking how she always maintained she would not live past the age of her own mother…83 years old. Three (3) days before Granny was to turn age 84, she was gone. Emotions overwhelmed me, yet I never expressed any.

Granny's death broke my heart, with sadness. I would not grieve for 3 years. I was unable to grieve because my maternal grandparents had 3 daughters; which of the 3 grandchildren, I am the youngest, and the only man-child.

Upon Granny's death, DaddyGreen had lost his life-partner of 65 years, having been married on October 28, 1950. DaddyGreen needed to grieve. My Mother, two (2) aunts, sister, and cousin would all need to grieve. In my mind, I would take time to grieve at the home-going celebration.

An issue would arise. At the wake, too many people were there for my comfort to grieve. The next day, at the funeral, the casket was closed.... My heart could have dropped. I was numb and full of emotion. I held it in, as it dawned on me I would never see my grandmother again.

I was unable to tell her how hard it was when my mom called me in the room, "Jonathan." The tone of her voice, I had never heard. I walked into the room. My mom's facial expression and emotion confirmed what I already knew. Granny took her last breath as I entered the room.

I heard her last breath leave her body, and her soul went with that breath, although I knew her spirit still resided within me. I know her spirit lives on in those she affected, positively; and God needed her in *Heaven*. I was not ready.

I was living life, going through the motions, again. Hastily, I quit my job at a local law office. After a few days, I had to ask for my job back. My employer showed some mercy, even though he typically was not a good man.

I say this because the particular attorney I was working for would yell and curse at his own mother, along with other employees, in the workplace. On a particular occasion, this attorney berated me. The strong, Black man, which my granny raised me to be was not having it. I went to that job for two (2) more weeks, and on the last day, I typed a letter of resignation, and left to vote in the 2016 presidential election.

I felt liberated, as I texted my new wife, "trust me." On October 1, 2016, my long-time friend,

Alexandria, and I were married. A month later, I was unemployed with a pregnant wife. My wife was an educator. Although I was not working, I would not allow for her to support me with financial obligations, despite her willingness.

As the holiday season approached, my wife and I went to a routine check-up at the doctor's office, being that she was pregnant. This visit, yielded us being in the hospital for weeks. The pregnancy became at-risk. My wife's life, and the life of our child, were in danger.

Langston Elizabeth entered into this world on December 15, 2016. Upon arrival, Langston Elizabeth's mannerisms reminded me of Granny. She even slept with one finger over her mouth. The pain of Granny's death was still present, but I obtained great joy at the birth of my daughter. This allowed me to become a father; and more importantly, become the father I did not have in my life.

## Chapter Thirteen

## Persist

Langston Elizabeth, whose middle name is the same as Granny's middle name, came a month and a half early. She helped renew a *part* of my life. I was a stay at home dad until August 2017, when I became an educator within the local school district. Finding employment proved difficult, being an over-qualified Black Man, with three (3) college degrees.

In 2017, I spent a majority of time influencing the upbringing of Langston, during her most formative time. I absolutely appreciated this time. That August, I began teaching social justice through reading. I was allowed to have seventh graders reading about the Black Panther Party through the books “Revolutionary Suicide,” and “The Assassination of Fred Hampton.” I was able to achieve this because I used these philosophies to facilitate classroom learning by having the students discuss how they can prevent bullying, using these techniques.

Also, in August of 2017, I was the victim of the *Water Bottle Case* in Pensacola, Florida. The incident occurred at the Confederate Monument Rally. I advocated the position against the monuments. An over 70-year old, white-man, named Alonzo Hicks, would hit me with a bottle of water, after acting like he was going to hit my mother. I stepped in to defend my mother. All this because he was upset I schooled him on the racist history of the United States, leading to his assault and battery, of my person. Alonzo Hicks would be found not guilty, 6-0, even with video evidence and witnesses.

The *Water Bottle Case* led to my 2018 candidacy for mayor of Pensacola, Florida. I ran to make a difference by being a voice of the unheard. Bringing up issues of poverty and injustice was vital to my platform. I learned a great deal about myself and about others. Also, I became a better public speaker. Around the time of the primary election, which I was not successful, My wife and I began to have more intense arguments, within our household.

# Chapter Fourteen

## When It Rains, It Pours

In May of 2017, one of my best friends, Garry, from the University of South Alabama would be deployed to the Middle East. In April of 2018, I was informed Garry would be having a return party in May. Being in this environment, I asked my wife of her past sexual relationships with any of the individuals we knew would be at this gathering. My question was based on her dishonesty in answering in the past. I wanted her truthfulness, to be able to continue developing a marriage of trust. I took her for her word in her response to me.

However, in July of 2018, a week prior to taking the bar exam a third time, a "friend" called to inquire about parking his car at my home. He would be flying out of Pensacola the day after me. However, this "friend" was one of the people mentioned by my wife as having a sexual encounter. I declined and went on about my business as usual. The day after returning from the bar exam, I called the "friend," asking if this was appropriate to ask me, given his past with my wife. He responded it was "probably fucked up." Also, he disclosed the true nature of their relationship.

The information disclosed revealed my wife lied, while looking me square in my eye. Even more disappointing, I asked her to be honest with me, on the strength of our marriage. She failed at being able to do so. She would spend the next 3 months maintaining her stance in her dishonesty, before admitting to her lying. However, she did much damage in her deep cutting words proclaiming my insecurity, while stating who she could have been with, instead of me. By November of 2018, my wife and I were separated; as she would demand I leave our home.

The year of 2019 was rough. I slept on the floor of a building I had access to, from January through April. In January, my wife would have my liberty taken through a Judicial Baker Act, which the doctors and case managers stated was a misuse of the courts. Our issues were domestic, not psychiatric nor psychological.

From April through June, of 2019, I would return to my marital residence, for sleep, because the night I took an air mattress to the building, I determined I was getting too comfortable in my houseless-ness. I informed my wife I would stay in the guest bed room, until the lease ended in June of 2019. This gave me more opportunity to spend time with Langston Elizabeth. My wife was agreeable.

On June 17, 2019, I was t-boned on my motorcycle. Being hit by a car hurts…a lot. Blessedly, I was not killed nor seriously injured.

My mom would help me begin to recuperate. My living in survival mode for months, led to my easily being irritable. My irritable state was due to my complex PTSD diagnosis. Eventually, my mom told me i was always using my PTSD as an excuse. This triggered me more because I was open, honest, vulnerable, and I allowed my feelings to be invalidated and minimized. I was hurt.

A good friend and fraternity brother, James, allowed me to sleep on his couch from August through November, of 2019. Some nights I slept in my truck because it was my own space. Every night I packed my bag, at James', and would take my bag with me each morning. This was in the event his generosity dwindled. I am glad to have met a true brother, and a generous friend, indeed.

At the end of November, I began to get my mind together, more so. I began more community organizing. Community rallies for justice, a holiday block party, and Breakfast on the Blocks was starting. Breakfast on the Blocks was where my comrades and I made egg/egg and cheese sandwiches, and then delivered the sandwiches to the projects and homeless camps on Saturday mornings. Moses Williams, owner of FatBoiz "A Real Sandwich Shop," allowed me and my comrades to utilize his business to make our sandwiches. A day after the first successful, Breakfast on the Blocks, things would take a drastic turn.

## Chapter Fifteen

## The Whirlwind

On January 5, 2020 Sergeant James Newton (#085), of the Escambia County Sheriff's Office, would violate my human rights and constitutional rights. Deputy James Newton responded to a call at a local Shell/Circle K Station, which I also called dispatch. My call to dispatch was to verify, whether a gas station manager called the police on me, for asking for corporate's number, after a disagreement about identification.

The deputy arrived, not knowing of my call to dispatch, where I outlined the sequence of events. Upon his questioning of me, after the gas station manager, Deputy Newton began to get irate. He was escalating.

My having been previously certified by the Florida Supreme Court in Circuit Civil Mediation, allowed me to have a certain set of skills, along with my experience gained as a Child Protective Investigator with the Florida Department of Children and Families. At this time, I was attempting to de-escalate Deputy Newton. I could not believe his inability to calm down, and his continued escalation.

At this time, I asked Deputy Newton "am I suspected of a crime, or am I free to go?" This statement infuriated Deputy Newton. He stated, "You are being detained so I can put you on the warning list for no trespassing." I then handed him my driver's license because his reason was valid. Once he took possession of my license, he stated “now you are under arrest for not leaving at my warning.”

Deputy Newton attempts to arrest me, which I place my hands in the air, while stating “what are your articulable facts to justify my arrest?” He forcefully places the handcuffs on me. While walking me to his patrol vehicle, he tells me “you can handle this in the court system.” Once I am on the blind-side of his police car, Deputy Newton slams me onto the side of his vehicle.

When my feet return to the ground, I yell “Help!” This pisses the deputy off, even more. I am then slammed into the middle of the parking space next to his patrol car, on his driver’s side.

Deputy Newton then places his left knee in the base of my skull, while pulling up on the person of my body, for the "search." I verbalize my pain, while narrating each of his illegal actions. He responds that my pain is, "good…."

Upon being placed in back of his patrol car, he illegally searches my parked vehicle, which i was not operating. However, he finds nothing as evidence because I have committed no crimes. Another officer arrives, soon after the escalation of Deputy Newton. I am transferred to the arriving deputy's vehicle, which I continue my protest. "What are your articulable facts to justify my arrest?"

In back of the second patrol car, I begin to have a manic episode, within the complex nature of my PTSD. I request medical assistance. It was determined I would go to the jail.

Upon being bailed out, I would go on a mental decline. That night, I informed my school's principal I would need to take a medical leave of absence. Seven days later, Pensacola Police would stop me and let me go from the detention, in my being a legal observer. I would begin to develop a paranoia at the sight of any law enforcement officer, or at the sight of a police vehicle.

Eleven days after the illegal arrest by Deputy Newton, I allegedly battered my mother, in a case of domestic violence. I had a psychotic break in reality, and my past mental health issues all contributed. However, Deputy Newton exacerbated my circumstances because I began to cope. I was developing good habits again, and had coping skills I was working on with my therapist.

I started therapy for the first time in August of 2019, where I was able to maintain consistency. I was only recommended to therapy in November of 2018. Deputy Newton set me back, completely. The seven (7) days spent in the Escambia County Jail were even more detrimental to my mental health. The only plus was the inmates, who helped me stabilize.

## Chapter Sixteen

## The Jail Cells of My Brain Cells

I told one of the arresting officers of my having PTSD. This message was not conveyed on my transport to the jail. I blacked out going into the sally port of the jail. The same tunnel vision as when I was on-line for my fraternity. A flash. I awake to being pulled out by my neck, on the driver's side of the car. I black out again.

I wake up, gasping for air. I am now on the passenger side of the vehicle, but I'm outside of the police car, on the cement. I ask myself, "How did I get here?" I realize I was gasping for air as I woke up because a corrections officer was choking me. A whisper in my ear, "you will not leave here alive." My head and neck are released.

My joints, bones and ligaments, are popping. There were people on my back, folding my arms and legs, while handcuffed. I begin to think, "there are at least four (4) people on me, and more are standing around. I really may die here." Sandra Bland immediately comes to my mind.

Being in good physical shape, I muster up all my strength and straighten my body's arms and legs. The officers go flying into the wall and on side of the police car. They come back with even more force. My joints are cracking even more. To stop them from breaking my bones, I had to state "yessuh Massa, I's'll be a good boy boss." After a few seconds,

I hear “that’s a good boy, as they place me in a restraint chair.”

Even the nurse did not show any concern or compassion. I insisted I needed help. None was given. They placed me in a suicide suit, and certain corrections officers often made homosexual innuendos. I was even placed in a suicide cell with high risks inmates. I would not receive medication for four (4) days. Once out of the jail, after six (6) days, I spent the seventh day in a hospital, under Baker Act. However, I was released later this day because of the inmates helping me stabilize, while confined in the jail.

## Epilogue

Since the initial arrest by Deputy James Newton, my mental health has been a constant work. I have two (2) psychiatrists and two (2) therapists. Each day is its own, and some are easier than others. One thing is for sure, these days are not the worst days of my past.

Ultimately, I took the Florida Bar exam 5 times. I Never properly prepared for the bar exam because of the lack of motivation to fulfill the purpose of a passion, not my own. Yet, I was taking the bar exam, attempting to fulfill a promise to Granny, in finishing what I started. I did not realize I had, until later.

Always remember to advocate for yourself because you can tell your story best. Be *Revolutionary*. And never be trapped inside your own mind. If you find yourself locked within, know your key resides within you too.

In the year of 2020, I have dedicated myself to having clear thoughts. These thoughts give rise to my clear vision. I have to love me, to love others. This allows one to do work to leave a legacy of everliving impact. This is the change Granny taught me. This is the change I live to effect.

Love yourself. Love others. Be blessed.